# Topic:

# LEVERAGING CUSTOMER RELATIONSHIP MANAGEMENT (CRM) FOR PERSONALIZED MARKETING STRATEGIES

By:

Sagar Wani & Ganesh Nemade

# Table Of Contents

# Introduction

In today's competitive business landscape, the key to success lies in understanding and catering to the individual needs and preferences of customers. Gone are the days of generic mass marketing, where companies would cast a wide net and hope to catch a few interested customers. The digital age has ushered in a new era of marketing, one that revolves around personalized experiences and meaningful customer relationships. And at the heart of this transformation is Customer Relationship Management (CRM).

The concept of marketing has evolved significantly over the years. In the early days, marketing messages were primarily delivered through mass media channels such as television, radio, and print. Companies would create catchy slogans and jingles, hoping to capture the attention of a broad audience. However, this approach often lacked the personal touch necessary to truly engage customers on an individual level.

As technology advanced and the internet became a ubiquitous part of our lives, marketing underwent a seismic shift. The rise of e-commerce, social media, and mobile devices opened up new avenues for businesses to connect with their target audiences. Suddenly, companies had access to vast amounts of data about their customers - their preferences, behaviors, and even their location. This wealth of information presented a unique opportunity to tailor marketing efforts to suit the needs of each individual customer.

This is where Customer Relationship Management (CRM) comes into play. CRM is a strategy and set of technologies that enable businesses to manage and nurture their relationships with customers. It goes beyond traditional marketing approaches by focusing on building long-term, personalized connections with individuals.

The importance of CRM cannot be overstated in today's business landscape. Customers have become more discerning and have higher expectations when it comes to their interactions with companies. They crave personalized experiences that make them feel valued and understood. In fact, studies have shown that personalization can significantly impact customer satisfaction, loyalty, and ultimately, the bottom line.

CRM allows businesses to gather, organize, and analyze customer data to gain a deeper understanding of their preferences, behaviors, and needs. With this information, companies can create highly targeted marketing campaigns, deliver personalized product recommendations, and provide tailored customer service experiences. By leveraging CRM effectively, businesses can build stronger customer relationships, increase customer retention, and drive customer advocacy.

Furthermore, CRM helps companies streamline their internal processes, improve collaboration among different departments, and enhance overall operational efficiency. It provides a centralized platform for managing customer interactions, tracking sales leads, and measuring marketing effectiveness. This not only improves the customer experience but also empowers employees to make data-driven decisions and deliver consistent messaging across all touchpoints.

In conclusion, the evolution of marketing has shifted from a mass marketing approach to one that emphasizes personalized experiences. Customer Relationship Management (CRM) is the driving force behind this transformation, enabling businesses to cultivate meaningful relationships with their customers. By harnessing the power of CRM, companies can unlock a treasure trove of customer insights, deliver tailored marketing strategies, and foster long-term loyalty. In the following chapters, we will delve deeper into the various components of CRM and explore how it can be leveraged to implement highly effective personalized marketing strategies. Get ready to embark on a journey that will revolutionize the way you engage with your customers and drive your business forward.

# Chapter One

# FOUNDATIONS OF CRM

## Defining CRM

Customer Relationship Management (CRM) is a strategic approach that focuses on building and nurturing strong relationships with customers. At its core, CRM is about understanding and meeting the unique needs and preferences of individual customers. It involves the systematic collection, organization, and analysis of customer data to enhance customer interactions and drive business growth.

CRM encompasses a range of activities, including customer acquisition, retention, and relationship development. It involves leveraging technology, processes, and strategies to optimize customer interactions across various touchpoints, such as sales, marketing, and customer service.

# Components of CRM

CRM is a multifaceted discipline that encompasses several key components. These components work together to form a cohesive system that supports personalized marketing strategies. **Here are the primary components of CRM:**

**Customer Data Management:**

Customer data management is a critical component of CRM that involves the systematic collection, storage, and management of customer-related information. This includes a wide range of data points such as demographic information, contact details, purchase history, communication preferences, and any other relevant data that helps businesses gain a deeper understanding of their customers.

Effective customer data management ensures that accurate and up-to-date information is available for analysis, decision-making, and personalized targeting. It involves establishing robust processes and systems to capture and organize customer data in a structured and accessible manner.

The first step in customer data management is the collection of data from various sources. This includes data obtained through customer interactions, such as purchases, inquiries, and feedback, as well as data acquired from external sources, such as market research, surveys, or social media platforms. Businesses may also leverage data enrichment techniques to supplement existing data with additional insights.

Once collected, customer data needs to be stored securely and efficiently. This typically involves the use of customer relationship management (CRM) systems or databases that provide a centralized repository for customer information. These systems ensure data integrity, enable quick access to relevant information, and support efficient data retrieval and updates.

To maintain data accuracy and relevance, businesses must establish data governance practices. This includes regular data cleansing, validation, and de-duplication processes to eliminate errors, inconsistencies, and duplicates. Additionally, data governance ensures compliance with data protection regulations and customer privacy rights, fostering trust and confidence among customers.

Customer data management also involves data segmentation and categorization. By organizing customers into distinct groups based on common attributes, businesses can tailor their marketing messages and strategies to better meet the specific needs and preferences of each segment. Segmentation may be based on factors such as demographics, purchasing behavior, engagement levels, or customer lifetime value.

Data management is an ongoing process that requires regular updates, maintenance, and monitoring. As customer data evolves over time, businesses must ensure data accuracy, completeness, and relevance. This may involve periodic data audits, data quality checks, and continuous data enhancement activities.

Overall, effective customer data management is crucial for successful CRM implementation. By collecting, storing, and managing customer data in a structured and secure manner, businesses can leverage insights to drive personalized marketing, enhance customer experiences, and build long-lasting relationships. Furthermore, robust data management practices ensure compliance with data protection regulations, fostering trust and maintaining the integrity of customer relationships.

**Sales Force Automation:**

Sales force automation is a key component of CRM systems that aims to streamline and optimize sales processes. It involves the use of technology and automation tools to support sales teams in managing leads, tracking opportunities, and automating routine tasks, ultimately enhancing their productivity and effectiveness.

One of the primary functions of sales force automation is lead management. It enables sales representatives to capture, organize, and track leads generated through various channels such as marketing campaigns, website inquiries, or referrals. CRM systems provide a centralized platform where leads can be stored, assigned to sales representatives, and tracked throughout the sales pipeline.

Sales force automation also facilitates opportunity management. It allows sales teams to manage and track potential deals or sales opportunities, providing a clear overview of the sales pipeline. Sales representatives can update the status of each opportunity, track the progress, and collaborate with team members to ensure timely follow-ups and actions.

Automation plays a crucial role in sales force automation by streamlining routine tasks. For example, CRM systems can automate email notifications, reminders, or task assignments, ensuring that sales representatives stay on top of their activities. Automated workflows can be configured to trigger specific actions or notifications based on predefined conditions, helping sales teams prioritize their efforts and manage their time effectively.

CRM systems often integrate with other tools and technologies to provide a comprehensive sales enablement solution. For instance, integration with email platforms allows sales representatives to send and track personalized email communications directly from the CRM system. Integration with calendar applications enables scheduling and managing sales appointments and meetings seamlessly.

Another important aspect of sales force automation is providing sales representatives with access to relevant customer information and sales collateral. CRM systems consolidate customer data, such as contact details, past interactions, purchase history, and preferences, ensuring that sales representatives have a comprehensive view of each customer. This information equips them with the knowledge needed to have informed and personalized conversations with customers, increasing the chances of successful sales conversions.

Moreover, sales force automation enables sales performance tracking and analytics. CRM systems capture data on sales activities, such as calls, meetings, or deals closed, providing insights into individual and team performance. These analytics help identify trends, evaluate sales strategies, and make data-driven decisions to improve overall sales effectiveness.

By leveraging sales force automation, businesses can streamline their sales processes, improve efficiency, and enhance the overall customer experience. Sales representatives have access to real-time customer data, automation tools, and analytics, empowering them to make informed decisions and deliver personalized and timely interactions. Ultimately, sales force automation contributes to increasing sales productivity, driving revenue growth, and strengthening customer relationships.

Marketing Automation: Marketing automation is a critical component of CRM systems that empowers businesses to streamline and optimize their marketing efforts. By integrating marketing automation tools, CRM enables targeted and personalized marketing campaigns that engage customers and drive business growth.

At its core, marketing automation automates repetitive marketing tasks, freeing up valuable time for marketing teams to focus on strategic activities. These tasks can include email marketing, lead nurturing, campaign management, social media scheduling, and more. By automating these processes, businesses can deliver consistent and timely marketing messages to their target audience.

One of the key benefits of marketing automation within CRM is the ability to leverage customer data to create highly targeted and personalized campaigns. CRM systems provide a centralized repository of customer information, including demographics, purchase history, communication preferences, and more. This data forms the foundation for creating customer segments and developing targeted marketing messages that resonate with specific audiences.

Marketing automation tools within CRM enable businesses to create dynamic email marketing campaigns. These tools allow for the personalization of emails based on customer data, such as first name, purchase history, or recent interactions. Automation features enable the scheduling and delivery of emails at optimal times, ensuring that customers receive relevant content when they are most likely to engage.

Lead nurturing is another key aspect of marketing automation. CRM systems facilitate the tracking and management of leads throughout the customer journey. By automating lead nurturing workflows, businesses can deliver personalized content and messages to nurture leads and move them closer to conversion. For example, based on customer behavior or engagement, automated workflows can trigger follow-up emails, recommend relevant content, or notify sales representatives to reach out to the lead.

Campaign management is streamlined through marketing automation within CRM. Businesses can create and manage multi-channel campaigns, including email, social media, and digital advertising, all from a centralized platform. Automation tools enable the scheduling and execution of campaigns, ensuring that messages are delivered consistently and in a coordinated manner across different channels.

Marketing automation within CRM also provides valuable analytics and insights. By tracking customer interactions, campaign performance, and lead conversions, businesses can gain actionable insights into the effectiveness of their marketing efforts. Analytics dashboards and reports provide metrics such as open rates, click-through rates, and conversion rates, enabling businesses to optimize their marketing strategies and improve ROI.

The integration of marketing automation within CRM enhances the overall customer experience. By leveraging customer data and delivering personalized and timely marketing messages, businesses can engage customers on an individual level. This personalized approach not only increases customer satisfaction but also improves the chances of conversion and customer loyalty.

In conclusion, marketing automation within CRM enables businesses to automate repetitive marketing tasks, deliver personalized campaigns, and optimize their marketing strategies. By leveraging customer data and delivering targeted messages, businesses can engage customers at the right time and through the right channels. Marketing automation within CRM contributes to enhancing customer relationships, driving lead conversions, and ultimately achieving marketing goals.

Customer Service and Support: Customer service and support are critical components of CRM systems that enable businesses to provide exceptional customer experiences and build strong customer relationships. By integrating customer service and support functionalities into CRM, businesses can effectively manage customer inquiries, support tickets, and issue resolution processes.

CRM systems offer a centralized platform for tracking and managing customer inquiries and support interactions. This allows businesses to capture and organize customer inquiries from various channels, such as phone calls, emails, social media, and live chat. By consolidating all customer interactions in one place, businesses can gain a comprehensive view of each customer's history and effectively address their needs.

CRM systems provide ticket management features that streamline the process of managing and resolving customer issues. When a customer inquiry or support request is received, a ticket is created to track and document the entire support journey. This includes information such as the nature of the issue, customer details, assigned support personnel, timestamps, and updates on the status and progress of the ticket.

Having a complete view of customer interactions and support tickets enables businesses to provide timely and effective resolutions. CRM systems facilitate collaboration and communication among support teams, ensuring that customer issues are assigned, escalated, and resolved efficiently. Support personnel can access customer information, previous interactions, and any relevant data to provide personalized and informed support.

CRM systems also enable businesses to set service level agreements (SLAs) and establish workflows for efficient ticket routing and resolution. SLAs define response times, resolution targets, and escalation procedures to ensure that customer inquiries are handled within specified timeframes. Automation features within CRM can trigger notifications, reminders, and escalations to ensure that SLAs are met and customers receive timely support.

Integration with other CRM modules, such as customer data management and sales force automation, enhances the customer service and support experience. Customer data stored in the CRM system provides valuable context for support personnel, enabling them to understand customer preferences, purchase history, and previous interactions. This contextual information allows for personalized and tailored support, demonstrating a deep understanding of the customer's needs.

CRM systems also facilitate knowledge management, providing a repository of information and resources that support personnel can access to address common customer issues. This knowledge base can include FAQs, troubleshooting guides, best practices, and other relevant documentation. Access to this knowledge base empowers support personnel to provide consistent and accurate information, ensuring high-quality support and minimizing response times.

Customer service analytics within CRM systems offer insights into support performance, including metrics such as response times, ticket resolution rates, and customer satisfaction scores. These analytics enable businesses to identify areas for improvement, optimize support processes, and enhance the overall customer service experience.

In conclusion, integrating customer service and support functionalities within CRM systems enables businesses to manage customer inquiries, support tickets, and issue resolution processes effectively. By having a comprehensive view of customer interactions and utilizing automation and knowledge management tools, businesses can provide exceptional customer service, foster customer loyalty, and drive customer satisfaction. CRM empowers businesses to deliver personalized and timely support, ultimately building strong and long-lasting customer relationships.

# Benefits of CRM for Personalized Marketing

Implementing CRM for personalized marketing strategies offers numerous benefits for businesses. **Here are some key advantages:**

Enhanced Customer Insights: CRM systems provide businesses with enhanced customer insights by analyzing and interpreting customer data. By leveraging the data collected within the CRM system, businesses can gain a deeper understanding of customer preferences, behaviors, and needs, enabling them to make informed decisions and deliver personalized experiences.

CRM systems offer powerful analytics capabilities that enable businesses to analyze and extract meaningful insights from customer data. By applying advanced analytics techniques, such as segmentation, clustering, and predictive modeling, businesses can identify patterns and trends within their customer base. These insights can help businesses identify different customer segments based on factors such as demographics, purchase history, engagement levels, and preferences.

Segmentation allows businesses to divide their customer base into distinct groups with similar characteristics or behaviors. By segmenting customers, businesses can tailor their marketing strategies, messages, and offers to each group's specific needs and preferences. For example, customers who have shown a preference for certain products or have specific buying behaviors can be targeted with personalized promotions or recommendations.

Clustering analysis helps identify similarities and differences within the customer base, allowing businesses to create customer segments based on behavioral or demographic attributes. This approach helps businesses identify hidden patterns and uncover valuable insights about customer preferences, enabling more effective targeting and personalized marketing.

Predictive modeling within CRM systems allows businesses to forecast customer behavior, such as likelihood to churn, purchase propensity, or response to marketing campaigns. By leveraging historical customer data, businesses can build predictive models that estimate future customer actions. These models provide valuable insights for targeted marketing campaigns and allow businesses to proactively engage with customers to optimize their experience and drive desired outcomes.

CRM systems also facilitate data visualization and reporting capabilities, presenting insights in a user-friendly and accessible format. Visualizations, such as charts, graphs, and dashboards, help businesses understand complex data patterns and trends at a glance. This visual representation of customer insights enables stakeholders to quickly identify opportunities and make data-driven decisions.

By leveraging the enhanced customer insights provided by CRM systems, businesses can design and execute highly targeted marketing campaigns. By understanding customer preferences, behaviors, and needs, businesses can create personalized messages and offers that resonate with individual customers. This level of personalization enhances the customer experience, increases engagement, and improves marketing campaign effectiveness.

Furthermore, CRM systems enable businesses to track the impact of marketing campaigns and measure customer response and engagement. By linking customer data to campaign data, businesses can evaluate the success of marketing efforts and optimize strategies based on real-time feedback. This closed-loop approach allows businesses to continuously refine their marketing initiatives, ensuring they align with customer preferences and drive desired outcomes.

In conclusion, CRM systems provide businesses with enhanced customer insights by analyzing and interpreting customer data. By leveraging these insights, businesses can understand customer preferences, behaviors, and needs, enabling them to create highly targeted marketing campaigns and deliver personalized experiences. By leveraging the power of CRM analytics, businesses can optimize their marketing strategies, improve customer engagement, and drive business growth.

Improved Customer Engagement: Personalized marketing through CRM systems enhances customer engagement by creating tailored experiences that resonate with individual preferences. By understanding customer needs and delivering relevant messages and offers, businesses can foster stronger connections with their customers, leading to increased customer satisfaction, brand loyalty, and advocacy.

Personalization allows businesses to go beyond generic mass marketing approaches and create customized experiences for each customer. With the insights gained from CRM systems, businesses can segment their customer base and deliver targeted messages and offers that align with specific preferences, interests, and behaviors. For example, a clothing retailer can send personalized recommendations based on a customer's past purchases or browsing history, suggesting items that are likely to appeal to their individual style and preferences.

By delivering personalized messages and offers, businesses demonstrate that they understand their customers and value their unique preferences. This level of personalization creates a sense of being heard and understood, fostering a deeper emotional connection with customers. Customers are more likely to engage with personalized communications as they perceive them as more relevant and meaningful.

In addition to tailored messages and offers, CRM systems enable businesses to engage customers through multiple channels, such as email, social media, mobile apps, and personalized landing pages. By leveraging these channels, businesses can create cohesive and consistent customer experiences across touchpoints, increasing the chances of customer engagement.

Furthermore, CRM systems facilitate timely and contextually relevant communications. By analyzing customer data and behaviors, businesses can identify key moments in the customer journey and deliver messages and offers at the right time. For instance, a travel agency can send personalized vacation offers to customers who have recently shown interest in specific destinations, increasing the likelihood of conversion.

The impact of personalized marketing on customer engagement goes beyond individual transactions. By consistently delivering personalized experiences, businesses can build long-term relationships with customers. Satisfied and engaged customers are more likely to become loyal advocates for the brand, sharing positive experiences with others and contributing to word-of-mouth marketing.

CRM systems also enable businesses to gather feedback and insights directly from customers, further enhancing engagement. By soliciting feedback through surveys, reviews, or social media interactions, businesses can demonstrate that they value customer opinions and actively seek to improve their products or services. This engagement fosters a sense of collaboration and co-creation, strengthening the relationship between businesses and their customers.

In conclusion, personalized marketing through CRM systems improves customer engagement by tailoring messages and offers to individual preferences. By demonstrating an understanding of customers' needs and delivering relevant experiences, businesses can foster stronger connections, increase customer satisfaction, and build brand loyalty. Through consistent engagement and personalized interactions, businesses can nurture long-term relationships and turn customers into brand advocates.

Increased Marketing Effectiveness: CRM systems empower businesses to enhance their marketing effectiveness by leveraging customer data and delivering personalized campaigns. By segmenting their target audience based on various criteria such as demographics, behavior, or preferences, businesses can create tailored marketing messages that resonate with specific customer segments. This level of customization ensures that the right message reaches the right customer at the right time, optimizing marketing efforts and driving better results.

One key aspect of CRM-driven marketing effectiveness is the ability to understand customer preferences and behaviors. By analyzing customer data captured within the CRM system, businesses can gain insights into individual customer needs, interests, and purchasing patterns. This data-driven understanding allows businesses to craft targeted messages and offers that align with customer preferences, increasing the relevance and effectiveness of marketing campaigns.

Segmentation plays a crucial role in delivering tailored marketing messages. CRM systems enable businesses to divide their customer base into distinct segments based on common characteristics or behaviors. For example, a clothing retailer might create segments for different age groups, style preferences, or geographic locations. By customizing marketing messages for each segment, businesses can speak directly to the unique interests and needs of specific customer groups, maximizing the impact of their marketing efforts.

CRM systems also facilitate precise targeting and personalization. By leveraging customer data, businesses can identify specific customer segments that are most likely to respond positively to a particular marketing campaign. This allows businesses to allocate marketing resources efficiently, focusing on the segments that offer the highest potential for conversion. Through personalized messages and offers, businesses can create a sense of individual attention, driving higher engagement and increasing the chances of conversion.

Furthermore, CRM systems enable businesses to track and measure the effectiveness of their marketing campaigns. By integrating CRM data with marketing analytics tools, businesses can monitor key performance metrics such as click-through rates, conversion rates, and customer acquisition costs. This data-driven approach allows businesses to evaluate the success of their marketing initiatives, identify areas for improvement, and make data-driven decisions to optimize future campaigns.

CRM systems also facilitate continuous improvement and iterative marketing strategies. By capturing customer feedback and response data, businesses can refine their marketing messages and offers over time. Through A/B testing and experimentation, businesses can identify the most effective marketing strategies and refine their campaigns based on real-time insights and customer feedback.

Ultimately, CRM-driven marketing effectiveness translates into higher conversion rates, increased customer acquisition, and improved return on marketing investments. By delivering targeted messages that resonate with specific customer segments, businesses can attract and engage customers more effectively, leading to greater customer satisfaction and long-term loyalty.

In conclusion, CRM empowers businesses to increase their marketing effectiveness by leveraging customer data, segmenting their target audience, and delivering tailored campaigns. By understanding customer preferences, businesses can create personalized marketing messages that resonate with specific customer segments. This data-driven and customer-centric approach leads to higher conversion rates, improved customer acquisition, and increased return on marketing investments.

Customer Retention and Loyalty: Customer retention and loyalty are crucial for the long-term success of businesses, and CRM plays a pivotal role in fostering these outcomes. Personalized marketing strategies enabled by CRM systems are instrumental in creating exceptional customer experiences that promote loyalty and encourage customers to stay with a brand.

Through CRM, businesses can gain a deep understanding of their customers' preferences, behaviors, and needs. By analyzing customer data and leveraging insights, businesses can tailor their marketing efforts to deliver personalized experiences that resonate with individual customers. This level of customization demonstrates to customers that their unique preferences and needs are valued, strengthening their emotional connection to the brand.

CRM systems allow businesses to track customer interactions across various touchpoints, including purchases, inquiries, and support interactions. By capturing and organizing this data, businesses can identify opportunities to engage with customers, provide relevant offers, and anticipate their future needs. This proactive approach to customer engagement helps to build trust and loyalty over time.

Personalized marketing efforts can take various forms. For example, businesses can send personalized emails with tailored product recommendations based on the customer's purchase history or browsing behavior. They can also create loyalty programs that reward customers for their repeat business or offer exclusive discounts and promotions based on the customer's preferences and past purchases. By tailoring the messaging, offers, and incentives to individual customers, businesses create a sense of personal attention and value, fostering customer loyalty.

Consistently meeting customer needs and expectations is another key aspect of CRM-driven customer retention and loyalty. By leveraging customer data, businesses can identify common pain points, address them proactively, and ensure that customers receive the support and assistance they require. This level of responsiveness and personalized service strengthens the bond between the customer and the brand, increasing customer satisfaction and loyalty.

Word-of-mouth marketing is a powerful driver of customer retention and loyalty. Satisfied customers who have experienced personalized and exceptional service are more likely to recommend the brand to their friends, family, and colleagues. This positive advocacy not only contributes to customer retention but also attracts new customers, expanding the brand's customer base.

Furthermore, CRM systems enable businesses to implement customer feedback mechanisms and gather insights on customer satisfaction and loyalty. By actively seeking feedback, addressing concerns, and incorporating customer input into business strategies, businesses can continuously improve their offerings and customer experiences. This iterative approach demonstrates a commitment to customer satisfaction and further strengthens customer loyalty.

In conclusion, CRM plays a vital role in fostering customer retention and loyalty. Through personalized marketing strategies, businesses can create exceptional customer experiences that resonate with individual customers. By consistently meeting customer needs, addressing pain points, and soliciting feedback, businesses build trust, loyalty, and advocacy. The result is increased customer retention, repeat business, and positive word-of-mouth, contributing to long-term business success.

Operational Efficiency:Operational efficiency is a critical aspect of business success, and CRM systems play a key role in streamlining internal processes and enhancing collaboration among teams. By providing a centralized platform for managing customer interactions, CRM facilitates the efficient flow of information and enables businesses to operate more effectively.

One of the key benefits of CRM is the elimination of data silos. With CRM, customer data is stored in a centralized database accessible to all relevant teams and departments. This means that sales, marketing, and customer service teams can access and update customer information in real-time, ensuring that everyone has the most up-to-date and accurate data. This eliminates the need for manual data transfer and reduces the risk of errors or inconsistencies.

CRM also promotes collaboration among teams by facilitating communication and knowledge sharing. With a centralized platform, teams can easily collaborate on customer-related activities, such as lead management, customer support, and cross-selling opportunities. This promotes a unified approach to customer interactions and ensures that everyone is aligned in delivering a seamless customer experience.

In addition to collaboration, CRM systems offer automation capabilities that streamline routine tasks and workflows. For example, CRM can automate lead assignment, follow-up reminders, and email marketing campaigns. This automation saves time and allows employees to focus on more value-added activities, such as building relationships with customers and closing deals. By automating repetitive tasks, CRM enhances operational efficiency and productivity.

CRM also enables businesses to track and measure key performance indicators (KPIs) related to customer interactions and business processes. By having access to real-time analytics and reports, management can identify bottlenecks, optimize processes, and make data-driven decisions. This improves overall operational efficiency by identifying areas for improvement and enabling continuous process optimization.

Furthermore, CRM systems offer customization and scalability options to adapt to the unique needs and growth of businesses. As businesses evolve, CRM can be customized to align with changing processes and requirements. Whether it's adding new fields, configuring workflows, or integrating with other business systems, CRM provides the flexibility to support evolving operational needs.

The improved operational efficiency achieved through CRM has a direct impact on customer experiences. With streamlined processes, businesses can respond to customer inquiries more quickly, provide accurate information, and deliver consistent messaging across various touchpoints. This leads to enhanced customer satisfaction, as customers receive timely and reliable service.

Overall, CRM systems enhance operational efficiency by eliminating data silos, promoting collaboration, automating routine tasks, and providing real-time analytics. By streamlining internal processes, businesses can work more efficiently, deliver exceptional customer experiences, and drive business growth. The result is improved productivity, cost savings, and a competitive advantage in the market.

***Conclusion:***

The foundations of CRM lay the groundwork for personalized marketing strategies. By defining CRM, understanding its key components, and recognizing the benefits it offers for personalized marketing, businesses can harness the power of CRM to build strong customer relationships, drive engagement, and achieve marketing success. In the following chapters, we will explore in-depth how to implement a CRM system, build customer profiles, leverage data analytics, automate workflows, and optimize strategies to deliver personalized experiences that truly resonate with customers.

# Chapter Two

# IMPLEMENTING A CRM SYSTEM

## Selecting The Right CRM Solution

Implementing a CRM system is a crucial step in leveraging customer relationship management for personalized marketing strategies. Choosing the right CRM solution is essential to ensure its effectiveness and successful integration within your organization. **Here are some key considerations when selecting a CRM solution:**

Identify Your Needs: Begin by clearly defining your business requirements and objectives. Understand the specific functionalities and features you need from a CRM system to support your personalized marketing strategies. Consider factors such as customer data management, sales force automation, marketing automation, and customer service capabilities.

When embarking on the journey of selecting a suitable CRM system for your business, the first and most crucial step is to identify your needs. This entails taking the time to clearly define your business requirements and objectives. By having a comprehensive understanding of what you expect from a CRM system, you can make an informed decision that aligns with your specific goals.

To determine the right CRM solution, it's essential to carefully assess the specific functionalities and features that will support your personalized marketing strategies. For instance, consider the significance of customer data management. Evaluating whether a CRM system can effectively capture, organize, and analyze customer information is fundamental for tailoring marketing campaigns and delivering personalized experiences to your clientele.

Another critical aspect to contemplate is sales force automation. Understanding whether you need a CRM system that automates various sales-related tasks, such as lead management, opportunity tracking, and pipeline analysis, is key to streamlining your sales processes and optimizing your team's performance.

In addition, ponder over the potential benefits of marketing automation. A CRM system that can automate marketing activities like email campaigns, lead nurturing, and customer segmentation can significantly enhance your marketing efforts, allowing for targeted outreach and improved campaign results.

Furthermore, consider the importance of customer service capabilities within the CRM system. Analyze whether the solution can effectively manage customer inquiries, complaints, and support tickets to ensure timely and satisfactory resolutions. A robust customer service feature fosters customer loyalty and strengthens your brand reputation.

By taking into account these factors, namely customer data management, sales force automation, marketing automation, and customer service capabilities, you can holistically evaluate the CRM systems available in the market. This assessment will guide you toward making a well-informed decision that perfectly caters to your business needs, empowering you to cultivate stronger customer relationships, streamline operations, and achieve your marketing objectives with precision and efficiency.

Scalability and Flexibility: Choose a CRM solution that can scale with your business and adapt to future needs. Consider the number of users, customer data volume, and potential growth. Ensure that the CRM system can accommodate your evolving requirements and integrate with other systems or applications.

In the quest for the most suitable CRM solution, it is essential to focus on its scalability and flexibility, ensuring that it can grow and adapt alongside your business. This consideration is crucial for making a long-term investment that remains effective as your business expands and evolves.

The scalability of a CRM system refers to its ability to handle increasing demands and accommodate growth. It is essential to assess whether the CRM solution can seamlessly scale with your business, both in terms of the number of users and the volume of customer data. As your organization expands, the number of users accessing the CRM system may grow, and it is vital to ensure that the system can handle the increased user load without compromising on performance or responsiveness.

Furthermore, with business growth comes an increase in customer data. A scalable CRM system should be able to efficiently manage and store larger volumes of customer information without slowing down or becoming cumbersome.

This ensures that your team can access and utilize vital customer data effectively, even as your customer base grows.

Flexibility is another crucial aspect to consider. A flexible CRM system can adapt and integrate with other systems or applications that your business may require in the future. As your business needs change or you introduce new tools and technologies, it is crucial that your CRM system can seamlessly integrate with these additions. This integration facilitates the flow of data across various platforms, enhancing data-driven decision-making and optimizing business processes.

Selecting a CRM solution that offers both scalability and flexibility sets the foundation for continued success and growth. It ensures that your CRM investment remains relevant and valuable, regardless of the changes and challenges your business may face over time. By choosing a CRM system that can scale with your business and integrate with other tools, you empower your organization to adapt and stay ahead in an ever-evolving business landscape.

User-Friendly Interface: The usability and intuitiveness of the CRM system are critical for user adoption and productivity. The interface should be user-friendly, with easy navigation, customizable dashboards, and intuitive features. Conduct demos and involve end-users in the evaluation process to ensure the system meets their needs.

The user-friendliness of a CRM system's interface holds significant importance, as it directly impacts user adoption and overall productivity within an organization. An intuitive and well-designed interface is essential for ensuring that users can easily navigate the system and make the most of its features.

The usability of the CRM system plays a pivotal role in how quickly and effectively users can accomplish their tasks. A user-friendly interface allows users to understand and use the system with minimal training or technical expertise. Clear and straightforward navigation menus and buttons are crucial, as they enable users to access various functionalities seamlessly, reducing the learning curve and enhancing efficiency.

Customizable dashboards are another valuable element of a user-friendly CRM system. These dashboards allow users to tailor their workspace, displaying the information most relevant to their roles and responsibilities. The ability to customize the layout and data display provides a personalized experience for each user, boosting their productivity by focusing on the information that matters most to them.

To ensure that the chosen CRM system genuinely meets users' needs, it is essential to involve end-users in the evaluation process. This can be achieved through demonstrations and gathering feedback from those who will be actively using the system. Including end-users in the evaluation helps identify any pain points or areas of improvement, ensuring that the CRM system is chosen based on real-world usage and practical considerations.

During the evaluation, it is important to observe how easily users can perform common tasks within the CRM system. Are essential features readily accessible? Is the workflow logical and intuitive? Addressing these questions during the evaluation phase allows organizations to make informed decisions based on how the CRM system aligns with their specific requirements.

In conclusion, prioritizing a user-friendly interface when selecting a CRM system is fundamental for user adoption and productivity. A well-designed and intuitive interface promotes efficiency, reduces training efforts, and increases user satisfaction. By conducting demos and involving end-users in the evaluation process, organizations can identify the best CRM solution that truly meets their needs and empowers their teams to achieve optimal results.

**Integration Capabilities:**

The integration capabilities of a CRM solution are a critical aspect to consider when choosing the right system for your business. Seamless integration with your existing systems, such as marketing automation tools, email marketing platforms, e-commerce platforms, and customer service software, is key to optimizing data flow and gaining a comprehensive view of customer interactions across multiple touchpoints.

Effective integration fosters a cohesive ecosystem where data can flow freely between different platforms. By ensuring that your CRM system integrates smoothly with other tools, you create a unified environment where all relevant data is consolidated, reducing data silos and minimizing the risk of inconsistent or outdated information.

For instance, integrating the CRM with marketing automation tools empowers your marketing team to access customer data directly from the CRM system, allowing them to craft targeted and personalized campaigns based on accurate customer insights. This seamless data sharing ensures that your marketing efforts are more efficient and that your messaging resonates with the intended audience.

Moreover, integration with email marketing platforms allows for seamless email campaigns, automated responses, and targeted lead nurturing, resulting in improved customer engagement and higher conversion rates.

For businesses with e-commerce platforms, integrating the CRM system can provide valuable insights into customer purchase history, preferences, and behavior. This information can then be leveraged by sales and marketing teams to better understand customer needs, anticipate trends, and tailor offers that align with individual preferences.

Customer service integration is equally vital, as it enables support teams to access complete customer records, view past interactions, and provide personalized assistance. This holistic view of customer interactions allows for faster issue resolution, enhanced customer satisfaction, and stronger customer loyalty.

In conclusion, the integration capabilities of a CRM system are essential for creating a cohesive and data-driven business environment. A well-integrated CRM system enables smooth data flow between various platforms, ensuring a comprehensive view of customer interactions. By considering how the CRM solution integrates with your existing tools, you can make an informed decision that enhances overall efficiency, improves customer experiences, and enables your business to thrive.

**Mobile Accessibility:**

In today's fast-paced and mobile-driven world, the importance of having a CRM solution with mobile accessibility cannot be overstated. It has become essential for businesses to ensure that their CRM system offers robust mobile capabilities, allowing their team members to access and update customer data on the go, irrespective of their location. This mobile accessibility enhances productivity, responsiveness, and overall efficiency, as team members can stay connected and engaged with critical customer information at all times.

A CRM system with mobile apps or a responsive web interface enables your team to access customer data, view important insights, and update records directly from their smartphones or tablets. This convenience is particularly valuable for sales representatives and field service agents who spend a significant amount of time on the road or meeting clients. With mobile accessibility, they can easily retrieve customer details, review recent interactions, and add new data in real-time, ensuring that they are well-prepared and informed during customer engagements.

Mobile accessibility also facilitates immediate responsiveness to customer inquiries and requests. Regardless of whether your team is in the office, at a client's site, or traveling, they can promptly address customer needs, provide relevant information, and address concerns without delays. This agility in response time can significantly enhance customer satisfaction and strengthen business relationships.

Moreover, a CRM system with mobile accessibility empowers remote or distributed teams to collaborate effectively. Team members can quickly share updates, coordinate tasks, and access real-time data, fostering seamless teamwork and communication even when team members are geographically dispersed.

Additionally, mobile accessibility plays a vital role in capturing time-sensitive information. For instance, during conferences, trade shows, or networking events, team members can instantly log leads, notes, and follow-ups, preventing any missed opportunities and ensuring that potential leads are promptly nurtured.

In conclusion, having a CRM solution with mobile accessibility is essential for businesses seeking to thrive in today's dynamic and mobile-driven environment. It enables your team to access and update customer data on the go, increasing productivity, responsiveness, and collaboration. With the ability to stay connected and informed, your team can deliver exceptional customer experiences and build strong, long-lasting relationships with clients, ultimately leading to business growth and success.

**Vendor Reputation and Support:**

Evaluate the vendor's reputation, experience, and track record in providing CRM solutions. Research customer reviews, testimonials, and case studies to gain insights into the vendor's performance and customer satisfaction. Additionally, consider the level of support and training offered by the vendor to ensure a smooth implementation and ongoing support for your team.

When considering a CRM solution, thoroughly evaluating the vendor's reputation, experience, and track record is a critical step to ensure a successful implementation and long-term satisfaction with the chosen system. The vendor's credibility can significantly impact the quality of service and support you receive throughout the CRM adoption process and beyond.

Start by researching the vendor's reputation in the CRM industry. Look for established and reputable vendors that have a strong presence and a history of delivering reliable CRM solutions. Online resources, industry publications, and customer forums can provide valuable insights into the vendor's standing within the market.

Customer reviews, testimonials, and case studies are excellent resources to gain firsthand perspectives on the vendor's performance and customer satisfaction. These sources offer valuable insights into how well the CRM solution meets the needs of real users and how satisfied they are with the vendor's services. Pay attention to recurring themes in customer feedback to identify any potential issues or strengths of the vendor's offerings.

Another crucial aspect to consider is the level of support and training provided by the vendor. A vendor that offers comprehensive support during the implementation process and ongoing assistance for your team ensures a smooth and successful adoption of the CRM system. Look for vendors that provide training programs tailored to your team's needs and skill levels. Adequate training ensures that your team can fully leverage the CRM system's capabilities and helps maximize its potential for your business.

Additionally, assess the vendor's responsiveness and availability for support and troubleshooting. Timely and effective support is essential in resolving any issues that may arise during the implementation or while using the CRM system in day-to-day operations.

In conclusion, evaluating the vendor's reputation, experience, and track record is vital to making an informed decision when selecting a CRM solution. Customer reviews and case studies offer valuable insights into the vendor's performance and customer satisfaction. Furthermore, considering the level of support and training provided ensures that your team can make the most of the CRM system, leading to a successful implementation and improved productivity in your business operations.

# Integration with Existing Systems

Successful CRM implementation involves integrating the CRM system with your existing systems to ensure seamless data flow and a unified view of customer information. **Here are some key points to consider when integrating your CRM system:**

Data mapping and data migration are crucial steps in the successful implementation of a CRM system. Properly identifying the data fields and entities that require synchronization between the CRM system and other applications is essential for seamless data flow and a comprehensive view of customer information.

To begin, assess the specific data fields and entities that your business needs to synchronize between the CRM system and other tools, such as marketing automation platforms, email marketing software, or customer support systems. Understanding the data elements that need to be shared ensures that all relevant information is available in both systems, avoiding data discrepancies and ensuring consistency across platforms.

Once the data fields and entities are identified, developing a data mapping strategy is critical to ensuring accurate data transfer. Data mapping involves establishing the relationships between data fields in different systems, mapping them to corresponding fields in the CRM system. This mapping process guarantees that data is correctly translated and synchronized, maintaining data integrity and coherence between systems.

An essential aspect of data mapping is to handle any variations or differences in data structure between the source systems and the CRM platform. By defining transformation rules and data conversion procedures, data mapping ensures that the data from various sources is effectively transformed and aligned with the required format in the CRM system.

Planning for data migration from existing systems to the CRM platform is equally important. A well-thought-out migration strategy helps avoid data loss, duplication, or inconsistencies during the transfer process. To minimize disruption to your business operations, consider conducting data migration during periods of low activity or during scheduled downtime, if applicable.

To ensure data integrity, perform thorough testing before and after data migration. This validation process helps identify and rectify any data-related issues before they impact your team's day-to-day operations.

Overall, careful data mapping and data migration planning are fundamental to a successful CRM implementation. By identifying the data fields and entities requiring synchronization, developing a data mapping strategy, and planning for a seamless migration process, businesses can ensure that their CRM system is fueled with accurate and reliable data, empowering their teams to make data-driven decisions and provide exceptional customer experiences.

The API and integration options of a CRM system play a crucial role in its adaptability and versatility. Evaluating these aspects is essential to ensure seamless data flow and interoperability with other essential applications used in your business.

A robust API (Application Programming Interface) is a key feature to look for in a CRM system. An API allows different software applications to communicate and share data with each other, enabling smooth integration between the CRM system and other tools. A well-designed API ensures that data can be transferred securely and efficiently, maintaining data integrity throughout the process.

When assessing the CRM system's API, consider its capabilities and flexibility. A comprehensive API should support a wide range of data transfer methods, including both one-way and two-way data synchronization. This means that data can be both sent to and retrieved from the CRM system, allowing for real-time updates and a comprehensive view of customer interactions.

Additionally, look for pre-built connectors or integration tools that the CRM system offers. These connectors act as ready-made bridges between the CRM system and commonly used applications, such as marketing automation platforms, email marketing software, or e-commerce platforms. Having pre-built connectors streamlines the integration process, reducing the need for custom development and saving time and resources during implementation.

The availability of integration options can significantly impact the CRM system's usability and its ability to work seamlessly within your existing technology ecosystem. By evaluating the API and integration offerings, you can ensure that the CRM system can be easily integrated with your preferred tools, enhancing data sharing and empowering your team to leverage the full potential of the CRM system.

In conclusion, the API and integration options of a CRM system are vital considerations in the selection process. A robust API and pre-built connectors facilitate smooth data flow between the CRM system and other applications, enhancing interoperability and simplifying the integration process. By choosing a CRM system with strong integration capabilities, businesses can build a cohesive technology environment, enabling data-driven decision-making and enhancing overall productivity and efficiency.

Customization and configuration are essential factors to consider when selecting a CRM system. These aspects allow you to tailor the CRM platform to match your existing workflows and processes, ensuring a seamless integration and a familiar user experience for your team.

One critical aspect of customization is the ability to adapt data fields to your specific business needs. A CRM system that allows you to customize data fields means you can capture and store information that aligns with your unique business requirements. By tailoring the data fields, you can record and track the data that is most relevant to your operations, enabling your team to work efficiently and make informed decisions based on accurate information.

Furthermore, customizing workflows is crucial to ensure that the CRM system complements your existing processes seamlessly. Your business likely has established workflows for sales, marketing, and customer service. A flexible CRM platform should allow you to configure these workflows within the system, automating repetitive tasks and streamlining your team's operations. This customization enhances productivity, reduces manual effort, and ensures that your team can work in a way that aligns with their established practices.

Reports are another area where customization plays a significant role. A good CRM system should allow you to configure reports and analytics to match your specific business requirements. The ability to create custom reports enables you to analyze the data that matters most to your business, providing valuable insights into customer behavior, sales performance, and overall business growth.

By customizing data fields, workflows, and reports, you ensure that your team can work with a CRM system that feels familiar and aligned with their way of doing business. A CRM solution that can be easily tailored to your needs helps overcome resistance to change and encourages widespread adoption by your team members.

In conclusion, customization and configuration are critical elements of a successful CRM implementation. Tailoring the CRM system to match your existing workflows and processes fosters a seamless integration and ensures a familiar user experience for your team. A well-customized CRM system empowers your team to work efficiently, make data-driven decisions, and ultimately achieve your business goals with ease.

Training and change management are critical components of a successful CRM implementation. To ensure user adoption and seamless integration of the new system, it is essential to develop a comprehensive training plan and effectively communicate the benefits of the CRM system to gain buy-in from employees.

The training plan should be well-structured and tailored to the specific needs of different user groups within the organization. Different teams, such as sales, marketing, and customer service, may have varying requirements, so providing targeted training ensures that each team can fully leverage the CRM system's functionalities for their respective roles.

The training sessions should cover various aspects of the CRM system, including navigation, data entry, reporting, and automation features. Hands-on training and interactive exercises can enhance user engagement and comprehension, enabling users to become proficient with the system quickly.

Furthermore, incorporating real-world scenarios and examples during training helps users understand how to apply the CRM system to their daily tasks and responsibilities. This approach allows employees to see the practical benefits of the CRM system, increasing their motivation to use it effectively.

Change management efforts play a significant role in the successful adoption of the CRM system. Clearly communicate the reasons for implementing the CRM system and how it aligns with the company's overall goals and vision. Emphasize the positive impact it will have on individual workflows, team collaboration, and customer interactions.

Address any potential concerns or resistance to change by involving employees in the decision-making process and addressing their questions and feedback. Demonstrating how the CRM system simplifies tasks, improves data accuracy, and enhances customer relationships can help alleviate apprehensions and gain employee buy-in.

Continuous communication and support after the CRM implementation are equally important. Encourage employees to share their experiences and best practices, fostering a culture of learning and collaboration. Regularly collect feedback and use it to identify areas for improvement and to provide additional training or support as needed.

In conclusion, training and change management are integral to the success of a CRM implementation. A comprehensive training plan tailored to different user groups, along with effective communication of the benefits, drives user adoption and ensures that the CRM system becomes an essential tool for the organization. By addressing concerns, involving employees in the process, and providing ongoing support, businesses can create a positive and supportive environment that embraces the CRM system and maximizes its potential for business growth.

# Data Management and Security

Data management and security are paramount when implementing a CRM system. Safeguarding customer data and ensuring compliance with privacy regulations build trust with your customers. **Consider the following aspects:**

Training and change management are critical components of a successful CRM implementation. To ensure user adoption and seamless integration of the new system, it is essential to develop a comprehensive training plan and effectively communicate the benefits of the CRM system to gain buy-in from employees.

The training plan should be well-structured and tailored to the specific needs of different user groups within the organization. Different teams, such as sales, marketing, and customer service, may have varying requirements, so providing targeted training ensures that each team can fully leverage the CRM system's functionalities for their respective roles.

The training sessions should cover various aspects of the CRM system, including navigation, data entry, reporting, and automation features. Hands-on training and interactive exercises can enhance user engagement and comprehension, enabling users to become proficient with the system quickly.

Furthermore, incorporating real-world scenarios and examples during training helps users understand how to apply the CRM system to their daily tasks and responsibilities. This approach allows employees to see the practical benefits of the CRM system, increasing their motivation to use it effectively.

Change management efforts play a significant role in the successful adoption of the CRM system. Clearly communicate the reasons for implementing the CRM system and how it aligns with the company's overall goals and vision. Emphasize the positive impact it will have on individual workflows, team collaboration, and customer interactions.

Address any potential concerns or resistance to change by involving employees in the decision-making process and addressing their questions and feedback. Demonstrating how the CRM system simplifies tasks, improves data accuracy, and enhances customer relationships can help alleviate apprehensions and gain employee buy-in.

Continuous communication and support after the CRM implementation are equally important. Encourage employees to share their experiences and best practices, fostering a culture of learning and collaboration. Regularly collect feedback and use it to identify areas for improvement and to provide additional training or support as needed.

In conclusion, training and change management are integral to the success of a CRM implementation. A comprehensive training plan tailored to different user groups, along with effective communication of the benefits, drives user adoption and ensures that the CRM system becomes an essential tool for the organization. By addressing concerns, involving employees in the process, and providing ongoing support, businesses can create a positive and supportive environment that embraces the CRM system and maximizes its potential for business growth.

**Backup and Disaster Recovery:**

Backup and disaster recovery are critical components of a robust data management strategy, ensuring data integrity, business continuity, and protection against potential data loss. By implementing regular data backups and a comprehensive disaster recovery plan, organizations can effectively mitigate the risks associated with system failures, hardware malfunctions, or natural disasters.

Regular data backups involve creating duplicate copies of critical data at scheduled intervals. These backups should be securely stored in separate locations, such as off-site servers or cloud-based storage, to protect against scenarios where the primary data storage becomes compromised. By having up-to-date backups, organizations can quickly restore data in the event of accidental deletions, data corruption, or cyberattacks.

A disaster recovery plan outlines the procedures and protocols to be followed in the event of a major disruption, such as a system-wide failure or a natural disaster. This plan includes predefined roles and responsibilities for key personnel involved in the recovery process, ensuring a coordinated and efficient response during stressful situations.

In addition to data backups, disaster recovery mechanisms encompass various strategies for data restoration. Organizations may use technologies like point-in-time recovery, where data is rolled back to a specific previous state, or continuous data replication, where data changes are automatically synchronized to a secondary location.

To ensure the effectiveness of backup and disaster recovery strategies, regular testing and validation are essential.

Conducting simulated recovery exercises allows organizations to identify any weaknesses or gaps in the recovery plan and take corrective actions. Testing also provides an opportunity to train staff on disaster response procedures, increasing the readiness of the team to handle real-life emergencies.

Furthermore, organizations should keep abreast of technological advancements and best practices in backup and disaster recovery. Staying informed about the latest security measures and data protection solutions enables businesses to continually improve their disaster readiness and data resilience.

Having a robust backup and disaster recovery plan instills confidence in stakeholders, customers, and partners. It demonstrates that the organization is proactive in safeguarding critical data and ensuring business continuity even during challenging circumstances. This proactive approach can enhance the organization's reputation and credibility, fostering trust among stakeholders.

Data security and privacy are integral to backup and disaster recovery. It is crucial to implement encryption and access controls to protect sensitive data both during storage and transmission. Compliance with relevant data protection regulations ensures that customer data is handled responsibly and in accordance with legal requirements.

In conclusion, backup and disaster recovery are indispensable elements of a comprehensive data management strategy. Regular data backups and a well-defined recovery plan provide organizations with the means to protect against data loss and swiftly restore operations in the face of disruptions. By investing in data resilience, businesses can safeguard their reputation, maintain customer trust, and effectively navigate unforeseen challenges in today's increasingly data-driven world.

**Data Retention and Compliance:**

Data retention and compliance are vital components of responsible data management practices. To ensure data protection and legal adherence, organizations must establish clear data retention policies that align with applicable laws and industry regulations.

Defining data retention policies involves specifying the duration for which different types of data will be retained. This includes customer information, transaction records, communication logs, and any other data collected during business operations. These policies should consider the legal requirements for data retention, such as data privacy laws, industry-specific regulations, and government mandates.

Customer data, in particular, requires special attention in data retention policies. Many jurisdictions have strict rules regarding the retention of customer data and explicit consent for its usage. Organizations must ensure that they comply with these regulations by obtaining proper consent from customers to collect and process their data, clearly informing them about the purpose of data collection and usage.

After the specified retention period, data deletion or anonymization processes should be in place to ensure that no data is retained longer than necessary. Secure data deletion involves permanently removing data from storage systems to prevent unauthorized access. Anonymization, on the other hand, involves removing personally identifiable information (PII) from the data, making it impossible to link the information back to specific individuals.

Implementing these processes requires careful planning and the use of appropriate technological tools. Data deletion and anonymization procedures must be designed to be irreversible and auditable, ensuring that no traces of the original data remain in the systems. Additionally, businesses must maintain detailed records of data retention and deletion activities for audit and compliance purposes.

To stay updated on the evolving landscape of data regulations, organizations should regularly review and adapt their data retention policies. Legal and industry requirements may change, necessitating adjustments to existing policies to remain in compliance.

Furthermore, employee training is crucial to ensure that data retention and compliance practices are followed diligently. Employees handling customer data should be aware of the legal obligations, the importance of obtaining consent, and the significance of secure data deletion after the retention period.

By prioritizing data retention and compliance, organizations can protect sensitive information, maintain customer trust, and avoid potential legal liabilities. A responsible approach to data management enhances the reputation of the organization and ensures that customer data is treated with the utmost care and respect. Overall, adherence to data retention and compliance requirements is an essential part of ethical and professional data handling practices.

**Regular Audits and Monitoring:**

Regular audits and monitoring are critical components of maintaining a secure and reliable CRM system. By conducting routine audits and continuously monitoring system activities, organizations can proactively identify potential security risks, detect suspicious activities, and ensure that their CRM system is up-to-date with the latest security measures.

Conducting regular audits involves systematically reviewing the CRM system's security measures, configurations, and access controls. Audits assess whether the implemented security measures align with industry best practices and comply with relevant data protection regulations. By performing audits at regular intervals, organizations can identify any security gaps or vulnerabilities and take corrective actions promptly.

Data access logs play a crucial role in monitoring user activities within the CRM system. By routinely analyzing these logs, businesses can track user interactions, access patterns, and usage behavior. Any anomalous or suspicious activities can be promptly identified and investigated to prevent potential security breaches.

In addition to data access logs, organizations should monitor system logs that record system events, errors, and user login activities. By monitoring these logs, businesses can proactively identify issues, such as failed login attempts or unauthorized access attempts, enabling them to respond quickly and take preventive measures.

Regular monitoring also involves analyzing user activities to detect any unusual patterns or potential security threats. By establishing baseline user behavior, organizations can spot deviations that might indicate security breaches or insider threats. Timely detection allows for immediate investigation and mitigation of potential risks.

Staying updated with security patches and updates provided by the CRM vendor is crucial for safeguarding the CRM system against emerging security threats. Vendors often release updates to address newly discovered vulnerabilities and enhance system security. Organizations should promptly apply these updates to ensure that their CRM system remains resilient to potential exploits.

To effectively conduct audits and monitoring, organizations should leverage advanced security tools and software that automate the process and provide real-time alerts for suspicious activities. These tools can assist in continuous monitoring and provide insights into potential security risks, empowering businesses to respond swiftly to threats.

Furthermore, it is essential to involve key stakeholders, including IT professionals and data security experts, in the auditing and monitoring processes. Collaboration between different teams ensures a comprehensive and holistic approach to CRM system security.

Overall, regular audits and monitoring are fundamental in maintaining a secure CRM system. By conducting audits, analyzing logs, monitoring user activities, and staying updated with security patches, organizations can enhance their CRM system's resilience, protect sensitive data, and fortify their defenses against potential cyber threats. Proactive security measures contribute to building trust among customers, partners, and stakeholders, assuring them that their data is handled with the utmost care and security.

***Conclusion:***

Implementing a CRM system involves selecting the right solution, integrating it with existing systems, and ensuring robust data management and security practices. By choosing a CRM solution aligned with your needs, integrating it seamlessly with existing systems, and prioritizing data management and security, you can lay a strong foundation for personalized marketing strategies. In the next chapters, we will explore how to build customer profiles, leverage data analytics, automate workflows, and optimize CRM strategies to deliver highly personalized experiences.

# BUILDING CUSTOMER PROFILES

## Gathering Customer Data

Building accurate and comprehensive customer profiles is essential for effective personalized marketing strategies. To create meaningful customer profiles, you need to gather relevant customer data. **Here are some key methods for gathering customer data:**

**Direct Data Collection:**

Direct data collection is a proactive and targeted approach that allows businesses to gather valuable information directly from their customers through various touchpoints. By employing customer registration forms, surveys, feedback forms, and preference centers, organizations can obtain specific and relevant data tailored to their unique business needs and preferences.

Customer registration forms play a crucial role in collecting essential information during the onboarding process. This data typically includes basic contact details, demographics, and preferences. By capturing this data at the outset, organizations can build comprehensive customer profiles, enabling personalized interactions and targeted marketing efforts.

Surveys are a versatile tool for direct data collection, allowing businesses to gather insights on customer satisfaction, product feedback, and preferences. Surveys provide a quantitative and qualitative understanding of customers' experiences, enabling organizations to identify areas for improvement and make data-driven business decisions.

Feedback forms provide immediate insights into customer opinions and experiences after specific interactions, such as making a purchase or engaging with customer support. Capturing feedback in real-time enables organizations to address concerns promptly and improve the overall customer experience.

Preference centers offer customers autonomy in managing their data and communication preferences. By allowing customers to opt-in or opt-out of specific marketing campaigns or select their preferred communication channels, organizations can ensure that their messaging aligns with individual preferences, enhancing the chances of customer engagement and loyalty.

The direct data collection approach offers several advantages. Firstly, it provides accurate and up-to-date information directly from the source – the customers themselves. This reduces the risk of data inaccuracies that might occur when relying on third-party data sources. Secondly, gathering data tailored to specific business needs ensures that marketing efforts and customer interactions are relevant and personalized, thereby increasing the likelihood of customer satisfaction and loyalty.

To make the most of direct data collection, businesses must consider data privacy and security. Obtaining explicit consent from customers before collecting their data is essential, as it ensures compliance with data protection regulations and fosters trust between businesses and customers. Implementing robust data security measures also safeguards sensitive customer information from unauthorized access and data breaches.

Moreover, direct data collection enables businesses to stay agile and responsive to customer needs. The ability to gather real-time feedback and preferences empowers organizations to adapt quickly to changing customer expectations, improve products and services, and develop targeted marketing campaigns.

In conclusion, direct data collection is a powerful and proactive method for gathering customer information. By employing various touchpoints like customer registration forms, surveys, feedback forms, and preference centers, organizations can obtain specific and relevant data tailored to their business needs and preferences. This data-driven approach enhances customer engagement, fosters personalized interactions, and supports data-driven decision-making, contributing to the overall success of businesses in a competitive market.

**Transactional Data:**

Transactional data is a treasure trove of valuable information that offers deep insights into customer behaviors, preferences, and purchase patterns. This data encompasses a variety of key elements, such as purchase history, order details, and customer interactions with a business's website or online platforms.

Purchase history forms the backbone of transactional data, providing a comprehensive record of every transaction made by individual customers. This data reveals the specific products or services purchased, along with the quantities, prices, and dates of the transactions. Analyzing purchase history helps businesses understand customers' preferences and interests, identify popular products, and anticipate future demand.

Order details provide a granular view of each individual transaction, including the specific items purchased, payment methods used, and delivery details. This level of information is invaluable for businesses seeking to optimize their product offerings, pricing strategies, and logistics processes. By analyzing order details, organizations can identify cross-selling and upselling opportunities and tailor their offerings to suit the needs of individual customers.

Customer interactions with a business's website or online platforms offer real-time insights into customer behaviors and preferences. This data includes clickstream data, navigation patterns, and engagement metrics. Analyzing customer interactions helps organizations understand how customers engage with their online platforms, enabling them to enhance the user experience, optimize website design, and improve conversion rates.

Moreover, transactional data can be leveraged for effective customer segmentation. By categorizing customers based on their purchase history and behaviors, businesses can create targeted marketing campaigns that address the unique needs and interests of each segment. This personalized approach increases the likelihood of customer engagement and fosters stronger customer relationships.

Transactional data also plays a crucial role in understanding customer loyalty and retention. By tracking repeat purchases and analyzing the frequency of customer interactions, businesses can identify loyal customers and develop strategies to nurture and retain them. Understanding customer behaviors and purchase patterns helps organizations implement loyalty programs and personalized rewards, further enhancing customer satisfaction and loyalty.

To leverage transactional data effectively, businesses must invest in robust data analytics tools and technologies. Advanced analytics allows organizations to perform complex analyses, such as customer lifetime value calculations, market basket analysis, and churn prediction. By gaining deeper insights from transactional data, businesses can make data-driven decisions, optimize marketing efforts, and drive revenue growth.

However, it is essential to balance the use of transactional data with customer privacy and data protection regulations. Organizations must implement strict data security measures and adhere to relevant data privacy laws to safeguard customer information and build trust with their clientele.

In conclusion, transactional data is a goldmine of valuable information that provides essential insights into customer behaviors, preferences, and purchase patterns. By analyzing purchase history, order details, and customer interactions, businesses can gain a comprehensive understanding of their customer base, tailor their marketing strategies, and enhance customer experiences. Leveraging transactional data in a responsible and data-driven manner allows organizations to stay competitive and build lasting relationships with their customers.

Online Tracking:

Online tracking is a powerful tool that allows businesses to collect and analyze valuable data on customer behavior across their website and other digital channels. By tracking various metrics, such as page views, click-through rates, time spent on each page, and abandoned shopping carts, organizations can gain deep insights into customer interests, preferences, and online behaviors.

Tracking page views provides a comprehensive view of which pages on the website attract the most traffic. By identifying the most visited pages, businesses can understand what content or products are popular among visitors, helping them optimize their website's structure and content to cater to customer interests.

Click-through rates (CTRs) measure the percentage of users who click on a specific link or call-to-action (CTA). Analyzing CTRs enables businesses to assess the effectiveness of their CTAs and identify areas where improvements can be made. By enhancing CTRs, organizations can drive more traffic to important pages or promotions, ultimately increasing customer engagement and conversions.

Time spent on each page is a valuable metric that reflects the level of engagement with website content. By tracking the time visitors spend on various pages, businesses can gauge the relevance and appeal of their content. Longer time spent on certain pages may indicate a high level of interest, while quick exits from other pages might suggest the need for content improvements or a better user experience.

Abandoned shopping carts are a significant concern for e-commerce businesses. Tracking and analyzing cart abandonment rates can help identify potential pain points in the checkout process or product offerings. Understanding the reasons behind cart abandonment allows businesses to implement strategies to reduce abandonment rates and optimize the conversion funnel.

Analyzing online tracking data provides organizations with a comprehensive understanding of customer preferences and online behaviors. This data-driven approach enables businesses to make informed decisions and tailor their digital marketing strategies to align with customer needs.

The insights gained from online tracking data allow businesses to create personalized customer experiences. By understanding customer preferences and behaviors, organizations can deliver targeted content, recommendations, and promotions that resonate with individual customers. Personalization enhances customer satisfaction, strengthens brand loyalty, and increases the likelihood of repeat business.

Furthermore, online tracking data enables businesses to conduct A/B testing and other experiments to optimize website performance and user experience. By testing different variations of web pages, CTAs, or product displays, organizations can identify the most effective approaches for driving conversions and customer engagement.

To ensure the responsible use of online tracking, organizations must prioritize customer privacy and data protection. Implementing transparent privacy policies and obtaining proper consent for tracking activities is essential to maintain customer trust and comply with data protection regulations.

In conclusion, online tracking is a valuable tool for businesses seeking to understand customer interests, preferences, and behaviors in the digital landscape. By analyzing page views, click-through rates, time spent on each page, and abandoned shopping carts, organizations can optimize their digital channels, create personalized experiences, and drive customer engagement and loyalty. When used responsibly and ethically, online tracking empowers businesses to stay competitive and deliver exceptional customer experiences in today's digital-driven world.

**Social Media Listening:**

Social media listening is a powerful strategy that enables businesses to tap into the vast amount of customer-generated content on various social media platforms. By monitoring and analyzing social media platforms, organizations can gain valuable insights into customer sentiments, discussions, and preferences, helping them to stay informed, engaged, and responsive to their target audience.

Monitoring social media platforms involves tracking mentions, comments, and conversations related to the brand, products, or industry. By actively listening to what customers are saying, businesses can gauge the overall sentiment towards their brand and products. Positive sentiments indicate customer satisfaction and brand advocacy, while negative sentiments highlight areas for improvement and potential issues that need addressing.

Analyzing social media discussions provides businesses with a direct line of communication with their customers. Understanding the topics and themes that customers are discussing allows organizations to identify trending topics, emerging issues, and popular opinions. This knowledge can be leveraged to shape marketing campaigns, create relevant content, and address customer concerns promptly.

Moreover, social media listening allows businesses to stay ahead of the competition by monitoring competitor activities and customer feedback about competing products or services. These insights help businesses understand market dynamics and customer preferences, enabling them to adapt their strategies and offerings accordingly.

Social media listening also offers a valuable opportunity for customer engagement. By actively participating in discussions, responding to customer queries, and acknowledging feedback, businesses can demonstrate their commitment to customer satisfaction and build stronger connections with their audience. Engaging with customers on social media fosters a sense of community and loyalty, encouraging customers to become brand advocates.

Understanding customer perceptions of the brand is another crucial aspect of social media listening. By analyzing customer sentiments and opinions, organizations can identify areas where the brand's image may need improvement or reinforcement. This awareness allows businesses to take proactive steps to shape their brand perception and reputation positively.

To effectively implement social media listening, businesses can utilize various social media monitoring tools and platforms. These tools offer real-time tracking and sentiment analysis, making it easier to capture and interpret customer feedback quickly. Automated alerts for specific keywords or mentions enable businesses to promptly respond to critical conversations and engage with customers in a timely manner.

Data privacy and ethical considerations are essential in social media listening. Businesses must handle customer data responsibly, adhere to privacy regulations, and obtain proper consent for data collection and analysis. Respecting customer privacy and data protection builds trust and fosters positive relationships with customers.

In conclusion, social media listening is a valuable practice for businesses seeking to understand customer sentiments, discussions, and preferences. By actively monitoring and analyzing social media platforms, organizations can stay informed about customer perceptions, identify trends, engage with their audience, and remain responsive to customer needs.

Social media listening is an invaluable tool for building brand loyalty, improving customer experiences, and staying competitive in today's dynamic digital landscape.

**Customer Service Interactions:**

Analyzing customer service interactions is a crucial aspect of understanding customer needs, pain points, and satisfaction levels. Customer service interactions encompass a wide range of communication channels, such as support tickets, live chats, and phone calls, which serve as valuable sources of data that can inform business strategies and enhance the overall customer experience.

Support tickets are formal records of customer inquiries, complaints, or requests for assistance. Analyzing support tickets allows businesses to identify recurring issues and pain points that customers encounter while using products or services. By tracking the types of tickets received and their resolution times, organizations can optimize their support processes, address customer concerns promptly, and improve overall customer satisfaction.

Live chats are real-time interactions between customers and support representatives. Analyzing chat transcripts provides insights into customers' immediate concerns, questions, and feedback. The data obtained from live chats enables businesses to identify common queries, fine-tune support responses, and implement improvements to streamline the chat experience.

Phone calls with customer service representatives offer an opportunity to understand customer emotions and sentiments more deeply. Analyzing call recordings and notes from these interactions can reveal valuable insights into customer pain points, emotional triggers, and satisfaction levels. Businesses can use this data to train their customer service teams, identify areas for improvement in handling customer inquiries, and enhance overall service quality.

By analyzing customer service interactions, businesses can identify patterns in customer needs and preferences. Understanding the common pain points and challenges faced by customers allows organizations to tailor their products, services, and support processes to meet those specific needs effectively. Addressing these pain points can lead to increased customer satisfaction and loyalty.

Customer service interactions also provide an avenue for gathering feedback and suggestions directly from customers. Organizations can use this feedback to make informed decisions about product enhancements, service improvements, and business strategies. Listening to customer suggestions demonstrates that the organization values customer input, fostering a sense of trust and loyalty.

Moreover, analyzing customer service interactions contributes to the identification of opportunities for process optimization and automation. By pinpointing frequently asked questions and issues, businesses can develop self-service options and knowledge bases, empowering customers to find answers on their own and reducing the workload on customer support teams.

To optimize the analysis of customer service interactions, businesses can leverage sentiment analysis tools. Sentiment analysis helps categorize customer feedback as positive, neutral, or negative, providing a more nuanced understanding of customer emotions and sentiments towards the brand.

In conclusion, analyzing customer service interactions is essential for gaining insights into customer needs, pain points, and satisfaction levels. Support tickets, live chats, and phone calls provide valuable data that can inform business strategies, improve support processes, and enhance the overall customer experience. By actively listening to customer feedback and using the data obtained from customer interactions, organizations can build stronger relationships with their customers and create products and services that better meet their needs.

**Third-Party Data:**

Incorporating third-party data into customer data is a strategic approach that can significantly enhance businesses' understanding of their target audience and improve customer profiling efforts. Third-party data refers to information collected and aggregated by external sources, such as data brokers, research firms, or other organizations, rather than being directly obtained from a company's own interactions with customers.

One of the primary benefits of using third-party data is that it enriches a business's existing customer data with additional insights and attributes that may not be readily available. Demographic data, such as age, gender, income, and geographic location, provides essential background information about customers, allowing businesses to create targeted marketing campaigns and tailor their offerings to suit the preferences of specific customer segments.

Consumer behavior data is another valuable type of third-party data that provides insights into how customers interact with various products and services. By analyzing consumer behavior data, businesses can understand buying patterns, brand preferences, and engagement levels across different channels.

This understanding enables organizations to optimize marketing strategies and deliver personalized experiences that resonate with their target audience.

Psychographic data, which includes customers' attitudes, values, interests, and lifestyle choices, offers a deeper understanding of customers' motivations and preferences. By integrating psychographic data into customer profiles, businesses can create more nuanced customer segments, allowing for more targeted messaging and personalized product recommendations.

Moreover, third-party data allows businesses to access information about potential customers who have not directly interacted with the company. This broader reach enables organizations to identify new market opportunities and expand their customer base.

Using third-party data also enables businesses to validate and enrich their own customer data. By cross-referencing their internal data with external sources, organizations can verify the accuracy of their records and gain additional context about their customers.

However, it is crucial for businesses to ensure the quality and reliability of third-party data sources. Not all third-party data may be accurate or up-to-date, so companies should carefully vet the data providers they work with and ensure compliance with data privacy regulations.

Data privacy and security are of utmost importance when dealing with third-party data. Businesses must handle this data responsibly, ensuring that customer information is anonymized and used in compliance with data protection laws. Transparent communication with customers about the use of third-party data is essential to build and maintain trust.

In conclusion, incorporating third-party data into customer data offers a wealth of benefits, including a broader understanding of the target audience and enhanced customer profiling efforts. By leveraging demographic, consumer behavior, and psychographic data, businesses can create more effective marketing strategies, deliver personalized experiences, and identify new market opportunities. However, organizations must approach third-party data integration with caution, ensuring data quality, privacy, and compliance to derive meaningful insights and maintain customer trust.

# Segmentation Strategies

Once you have gathered customer data, the next step is to segment your customer base. Segmentation allows you to categorize customers into distinct groups based on shared characteristics, behaviors, or preferences. Here are some segmentation strategies to consider:

Demographic Segmentation: Segment customers based on demographic variables such as age, gender, income, occupation, or location. Demographic segmentation provides a basic understanding of customer groups and helps tailor marketing messages accordingly.

Psychographic Segmentation: This approach segments customers based on their attitudes, beliefs, values, lifestyles, and interests. Psychographic segmentation delves deeper into customers' motivations and preferences, enabling more targeted and relevant marketing strategies.

Behavioral Segmentation: Segment customers based on their behaviors, such as purchase history, frequency of purchases, product usage, or engagement levels. Behavioral segmentation helps identify customer segments with similar purchase patterns and allows for personalized offers or recommendations.

Customer Lifecycle Segmentation: Divide customers based on their stage in the customer lifecycle, such as prospects, first-time buyers, repeat buyers, or loyal customers. This segmentation allows you to tailor marketing strategies specific to each stage and nurture customer relationships accordingly.

Persona Development: Develop customer personas, which are fictional representations of your ideal customers. Personas are created based on a combination of demographic, psychographic, and behavioral data. Personas humanize customer segments and help guide marketing strategies by understanding customers' motivations, needs, and pain points.

# Creating Comprehensive Customer Profiles

Creating comprehensive customer profiles involves synthesizing the gathered data and segmentation insights into detailed customer profiles. **Here are some key steps to create comprehensive customer profiles:**

Consolidate Data: Consolidate customer data from various sources into a centralized database or CRM system. Ensure data accuracy, completeness, and data hygiene by removing duplicates, validating information, and updating outdated records.

Develop Customer Profile Fields: Determine the essential profile fields that capture relevant customer information. This can include demographic data, psychographic traits, behavioral patterns, purchase history, communication preferences, and customer interactions. Customize profile fields based on your business needs and segmentation strategy.

Analyze Data Patterns: Analyze customer data to identify patterns, trends, and insights. Look for commonalities among customer segments, such as preferences for specific products, preferred communication channels, or response patterns to marketing campaigns. These insights will help tailor marketing strategies for each customer profile.

Customer Journey Mapping: Map out the customer journey and touchpoints across different channels and stages. Identify key interactions, pain points, and opportunities for personalized engagement. This mapping helps create personalized experiences at each stage of the customer journey.

Continuously Update Profiles: Regularly update customer profiles with new data and insights. Customer preferences and behaviors can change over time, so it's important to keep profiles up to date to maintain the relevance of your marketing strategies.

***Conclusion:***

Building customer profiles is a crucial step in personalized marketing strategies. By gathering relevant customer data, implementing segmentation strategies, and creating comprehensive customer profiles, you can tailor your marketing efforts to meet individual customer needs, preferences, and behaviors. In the next chapters, we will explore how to leverage data analytics, automate workflows, and optimize CRM strategies to deliver highly personalized marketing campaigns.

# Chapter Four

# LEVERAGING CRM FOR PERSONALIZATION

## Customizing Product Recommendations

One of the key benefits of CRM for personalized marketing is the ability to provide customized product recommendations to customers. By leveraging customer data and insights from CRM systems, businesses can create personalized recommendations that align with individual preferences and increase the likelihood of purchase. **Here are some strategies for customizing product recommendations:**

Collaborative Filtering: Implement collaborative filtering techniques to recommend products based on the purchasing behaviors and preferences of similar customers. By analyzing past purchase data, CRM systems can identify patterns and recommend products that customers with similar profiles have shown interest in.

Cross-Selling and Upselling: Utilize CRM data to identify opportunities for cross-selling and upselling. Analyze customer purchase history to understand related products or higher-priced alternatives that may complement their previous purchases. Use this information to present personalized recommendations during the customer journey.

Personalized Landing Pages: Create personalized landing pages that display recommended products based on a customer's browsing history, purchase history, or preferences. By tailoring the content and product offerings to individual customers, businesses can enhance the relevance and effectiveness of their marketing campaigns.

Dynamic Email Recommendations: Leverage CRM data to generate dynamic email content that includes personalized product recommendations. Use customer segmentation and purchase history to send targeted emails with recommended products that align with individual preferences and buying habits.

# Tailoring Marketing Messages

CRM systems enable businesses to tailor marketing messages to individual customers, increasing engagement and conversion rates. By leveraging customer data and insights, businesses can deliver targeted and relevant messages that resonate with their audience. **Here are some strategies for tailoring marketing messages:**

Personalized Email Campaigns: Use CRM data to segment customers and create personalized email campaigns. Customize email content based on customer preferences, demographics, or past interactions. Incorporate dynamic content and personalization tokens to address customers by name and provide relevant offers or recommendations.

Behavioral Triggers: Set up automated behavioral triggers based on customer actions or interactions. For example, if a customer abandons a shopping cart, send them a personalized email reminder with a special discount. These triggered messages demonstrate attentiveness and encourage customers to complete their purchase.

Contextual Advertising: Utilize CRM data to create targeted advertising campaigns across various channels. Use customer segmentation and preferences to display relevant ads that align with individual interests and needs. By tailoring advertising messages, businesses can improve click-through rates and conversions.

Social Media Personalization: Leverage CRM data to personalize social media marketing efforts. Create custom audiences and deliver tailored content, offers, or ads on platforms like Facebook, Instagram, or LinkedIn. Align the messaging with customer preferences, behaviors, or demographics to increase engagement and brand affinity.

# Enhancing The Customer Experience

CRM systems play a crucial role in enhancing the overall customer experience. By leveraging customer data and insights, businesses can deliver personalized experiences that meet individual needs and foster loyalty. **Here are some strategies to enhance the customer experience using CRM:**

**Omnichannel Engagement:** Use CRM data to provide a seamless omnichannel experience to customers. Ensure consistent messaging, personalization, and customer service across various touchpoints, such as website, mobile apps, social media, and offline interactions. This integrated approach builds trust and loyalty among customers.

Proactive Customer Service: Leverage CRM data to provide proactive customer service. Anticipate customer needs and issues based on past interactions or purchase history. Implement proactive customer outreach, such as personalized follow-up emails or notifications, to address concerns before they escalate.

Personalized Support: Equip customer service representatives with comprehensive customer profiles and relevant data. This empowers them to provide personalized support, resolve issues efficiently, and offer tailored solutions. Personalized support demonstrates a deep understanding of customers and enhances their overall experience.

**Loyalty Programs and Rewards:** Use CRM data to identify loyal customers and create personalized loyalty programs. Offer rewards, exclusive discounts, or special perks based on customer preferences and purchase history. Tailor loyalty program benefits to individual customers to strengthen their engagement and repeat purchases.

*Conclusion:*

Leveraging CRM for personalized marketing strategies empowers businesses to deliver customized product recommendations, tailor marketing messages, and enhance the overall customer experience. By leveraging customer data and insights from CRM systems, businesses can create meaningful interactions, foster customer loyalty, and drive revenue growth. In the next chapters, we will explore how to automate workflows and optimize CRM strategies to further enhance personalized marketing efforts.

# Chapter Five

# HARNESSING DATA ANALYTICS

## Analyzing Customer Behavior

Data analytics plays a critical role in leveraging customer relationship management (CRM) for personalized marketing strategies. By analyzing customer behavior, businesses can gain valuable insights into their preferences, habits, and needs. **Here are some key aspects of analyzing customer behavior:**

**Data Mining:** Utilize data mining techniques to extract meaningful patterns and insights from customer data. Analyze historical data, such as purchase history, website interactions, and social media engagements, to identify trends, preferences, and behavior patterns.

Segmentation Analysis: Conduct in-depth segmentation analysis to understand the characteristics and behaviors of different customer segments. Identify commonalities, preferences, and purchase patterns within each segment. This analysis enables businesses to tailor marketing strategies specifically for each segment.

Customer Journey Mapping: Map out the customer journey across various touchpoints and channels. Analyze customer interactions, behaviors, and touchpoint effectiveness at each stage. This mapping helps identify pain points, opportunities for personalization, and areas for improvement in the customer experience.

Cohort Analysis: Perform cohort analysis to examine customer groups with similar characteristics or behaviors over a specific time frame. This analysis helps uncover trends, understand customer retention rates, and identify opportunities to optimize marketing efforts for specific cohorts.

# Predictive Analytics for Personalization

Predictive analytics allows businesses to forecast future customer behaviors and preferences, enabling personalized marketing strategies. By leveraging historical data and advanced analytics techniques, businesses can anticipate customer needs and deliver proactive personalized experiences. **Here are some ways to harness predictive analytics for personalization:**

Customer Lifetime Value (CLV) Prediction: Predict the potential value of each customer over their lifetime using predictive models. CLV prediction helps prioritize marketing efforts, tailor offers, and allocate resources to high-value customers, fostering customer loyalty and maximizing revenue.

Churn Prediction: Utilize predictive analytics to identify customers at risk of churning or discontinuing their relationship with the business. By detecting early warning signs, businesses can take proactive measures, such as targeted retention campaigns or personalized offers, to prevent customer churn.

Next Best Offer Prediction: Predict the most relevant and appealing offers for individual customers based on their preferences, past purchases, and behavior patterns. By leveraging predictive models, businesses can provide personalized recommendations that increase the likelihood of conversion and customer satisfaction.

Personalized Content Recommendations: Utilize predictive analytics to recommend personalized content to customers. Analyze historical data, such as content consumption patterns or browsing behavior, to anticipate customer interests and deliver tailored content recommendations.

# Using CRM Insights to Drive Marketing Decisions

CRM systems generate a wealth of insights that can drive strategic marketing decisions. By leveraging CRM insights, businesses can make data-driven decisions to optimize marketing efforts and deliver personalized experiences. **Here are some ways to use CRM insights for marketing decisions:**

Marketing Campaign Optimization: Analyze CRM data to evaluate the performance of marketing campaigns. Measure key metrics such as click-through rates, conversion rates, and customer engagement. Identify successful campaign elements and areas for improvement to optimize future marketing initiatives.

Personalization Strategy Refinement: Leverage CRM insights to refine and enhance personalization strategies. Monitor customer responses, feedback, and satisfaction levels to gauge the effectiveness of personalization efforts. Continuously analyze CRM data to identify opportunities for further customization and personalization.

Customer Segmentation Refinement: Use CRM insights to refine customer segmentation strategies. Analyze customer data and behaviors to identify new segments or modify existing ones. Continuously evaluate the effectiveness of segmentation in delivering personalized experiences and adjust as needed.

Customer Lifetime Value Analysis: Utilize CRM insights to assess the lifetime value of different customer segments. Identify segments with higher profitability, customer loyalty, or growth potential. Allocate marketing resources and investment based on customer segment priorities.

### *Conclusion:*

Harnessing data analytics in conjunction with CRM enables businesses to analyze customer behavior, utilize predictive analytics for personalization, and make data-driven marketing decisions. By leveraging insights from CRM systems, businesses can optimize marketing campaigns, refine personalization strategies, and deliver exceptional customer experiences. In the next chapters, we will explore workflow automation and CRM optimization techniques to further enhance personalized marketing strategies.

# Chapter Six

# AUTOMATION AND WORKFLOW OPTIMIZATION

## Streamlining Marketing Processes

Streamlining marketing processes is essential for efficient and effective personalized marketing strategies. By automating repetitive tasks and optimizing workflows, businesses can save time, reduce errors, and increase productivity. **Here are some ways to streamline marketing processes:**

Marketing Workflow Mapping: Map out your marketing workflows to identify bottlenecks, redundancies, and areas for improvement. Analyze each step of the process, from campaign planning to execution and reporting. Streamline workflows by removing unnecessary steps, automating manual tasks, and optimizing the sequence of activities.

Marketing Technology Integration: Integrate your CRM system with other marketing technologies, such as email marketing platforms, social media management tools, or content management systems. This integration enables seamless data flow, eliminates manual data entry, and enhances collaboration across teams.

Centralized Marketing Calendar: Maintain a centralized marketing calendar that encompasses all marketing activities, campaigns, and deadlines. This calendar provides visibility into upcoming campaigns, avoids scheduling conflicts, and allows for better resource allocation and planning.

Collaboration and Communication Tools: Utilize collaboration and communication tools, such as project management software or team collaboration platforms, to streamline communication and task management. These tools enable real-time collaboration, task assignment, and progress tracking, ensuring efficient workflow management.

# Automated Campaign Management

Automating campaign management processes can significantly enhance personalized marketing strategies. By leveraging CRM automation features, businesses can execute campaigns more efficiently, deliver targeted messages, and track performance effectively. **Here are some aspects of automated campaign management:**

**Triggered Campaigns:** Set up triggered campaigns based on predefined customer actions or events. For example, automatically send a welcome email series to new subscribers or follow-up emails after a customer makes a purchase. Triggered campaigns ensure timely and relevant communication, increasing engagement and conversion rates.

Personalized Email Automation: Utilize CRM data and automation tools to create personalized email campaigns. Develop email templates with dynamic content that pulls information from customer profiles, such as name, purchase history, or recommended products. Automate email sends based on specific customer segments or triggers.

Drip Campaigns: Implement drip campaigns to deliver a series of automated, targeted messages over time. Use CRM insights to segment customers and deliver personalized content at different stages of the customer journey. Drip campaigns nurture customer relationships, build engagement, and drive conversions.

A/B Testing and Optimization: Leverage automation tools to conduct A/B testing and optimize campaign elements. Test different subject lines, content variations, or calls-to-action to identify the most effective messaging. Automate the testing process and analyze results to continually improve campaign performance.

# Workflow Automation for Efficient CRM

Workflow automation within CRM systems streamlines processes, improves data accuracy, and enhances overall efficiency. By automating routine tasks and ensuring data consistency, businesses can focus on delivering personalized experiences. **Here are some workflow automation strategies for efficient CRM:**

Lead Management Automation: Automate lead management processes, including lead capture, assignment, and nurturing. Use CRM workflows to automatically assign leads to appropriate sales or marketing teams based on predefined criteria. Implement lead scoring models to prioritize leads and trigger personalized nurturing campaigns.

Customer Onboarding and Engagement: Automate customer onboarding processes to ensure a smooth and personalized experience. Use CRM workflows to send welcome emails, guide customers through onboarding steps, and deliver relevant content based on their interests or purchase history. Automated onboarding enhances customer satisfaction and reduces churn.

Data Enrichment and Validation: Implement automated data enrichment and validation processes within CRM systems. Use integration with external data sources to update customer profiles with accurate and up-to-date information. Automate data validation checks to maintain data integrity and minimize errors in customer records.

Reporting and Analytics Automation: Automate reporting and analytics processes to gain real-time insights into campaign performance, customer engagement, and ROI. Use CRM reporting features or integration with analytics tools to generate customized reports, dashboards, and visualizations. Automated reporting saves time and provides actionable insights for decision-making.

***Conclusion:***

Automation and workflow optimization are crucial for streamlining marketing processes, automating campaign management, and ensuring efficient CRM operations. By leveraging automation tools within CRM systems, businesses can enhance productivity, deliver personalized experiences, and improve data accuracy. In the next chapter, we will explore CRM optimization techniques to maximize the value of customer relationship management for personalized marketing strategies.

# Chapter Seven

# THE POWER OF OMNICHANNEL MARKETING

## Integrating Multiple Channels

In today's digital landscape, customers interact with brands through various channels, both online and offline. To deliver seamless personalized marketing experiences, businesses must integrate multiple channels within their customer relationship management (CRM) strategies. **Here's how to integrate multiple channels effectively:**

Channel Mapping: Identify the key channels your customers use to engage with your brand. This may include websites, social media platforms, email, mobile apps, physical stores, and more. Map out the customer journey across these channels to understand how customers move between them.

Data Integration: Ensure data integration across channels by connecting various systems and platforms to your CRM system. This allows for a unified view of customer data, preferences, and interactions. Integrating data from different channels enables personalized marketing efforts based on a comprehensive understanding of customer behavior.

Cross-Channel Tracking: Implement cross-channel tracking to monitor customer interactions and behavior across various touchpoints. This allows you to gather valuable data and insights on customer preferences, engagement patterns, and purchasing behavior. Cross-channel tracking enables the delivery of consistent and personalized experiences.

# Creating Consistent Customer Experiences

Consistency is key in delivering personalized marketing experiences. Customers expect a seamless and consistent experience, regardless of the channel they are using. **Here's how to create consistent customer experiences:**

Branding and Messaging: Ensure consistent branding and messaging across all channels. Use the same visual elements, tone of voice, and value propositions to maintain a cohesive brand identity. Consistent branding and messaging reinforce customer recognition and trust.

Personalization Across Channels: Extend personalization efforts across all channels to create a consistent experience. Leverage CRM data to deliver relevant and tailored content, product recommendations, and offers through each customer touchpoint. Consistent personalization enhances customer engagement and satisfaction.

Responsive Design: Optimize your digital channels, such as websites and emails, for a responsive design. This ensures a consistent user experience across different devices and screen sizes. Responsive design enables customers to interact with your brand seamlessly, regardless of the device they use.

## Orchestrating Personalized Campaigns

Omnichannel marketing allows businesses to orchestrate personalized campaigns that engage customers at every stage of their journey. **Here's how to orchestrate personalized campaigns effectively:**

Customer Segmentation: Leverage CRM data to segment your customers based on their preferences, behaviors, demographics, or purchase history. Use these segments to create targeted campaigns that resonate with specific customer groups. Personalized campaigns increase relevance and drive higher engagement.

Automated Journey Workflows: Implement automated journey workflows to guide customers through personalized experiences across channels. Define the touchpoints, content, and interactions that customers will encounter at each stage of their journey. Automated workflows ensure consistent and timely engagement with personalized messaging.

Dynamic Content Personalization: Utilize dynamic content personalization techniques to deliver customized content to customers. Tailor the content based on customer preferences, behaviors, or interactions. Dynamic content personalization increases engagement and conversion rates by providing customers with relevant and timely information.

Marketing Automation Platforms: Invest in marketing automation platforms that integrate with your CRM system. These platforms enable you to automate campaign execution, track customer interactions, and measure campaign performance across multiple channels. Marketing automation platforms streamline personalized campaign management and optimization.

### *Conclusion:*

Omnichannel marketing is a powerful approach to deliver personalized experiences to customers. By integrating multiple channels, creating consistent customer experiences, and orchestrating personalized campaigns, businesses can engage customers at every touchpoint and foster long-term relationships. In the final chapter, we will summarize the key takeaways and discuss the future of personalized marketing strategies with CRM.

## Chapter Eight

# PERSONALIZATION AT SCALE

## Managing Large Customer Databases

As businesses grow and acquire a larger customer base, managing large customer databases becomes crucial for effective personalized marketing strategies. **Here are some key considerations for managing large customer databases:**

Data Organization: Implement a robust data organization strategy to efficiently store and manage customer data. Use CRM systems with advanced database management capabilities to organize customer profiles, preferences, purchase history, and other relevant data points. Proper data organization ensures easy access and retrieval of customer information.

Data Cleansing and Maintenance: Regularly clean and maintain your customer database to ensure data accuracy and integrity. Remove duplicate records, update outdated information, and validate data to eliminate errors. Implement data quality checks and establish protocols for ongoing data maintenance.

Scalable Infrastructure: Ensure that your CRM infrastructure is scalable and capable of handling large volumes of customer data. Consider cloud-based CRM solutions that offer flexibility and scalability as your customer database grows. Scalable infrastructure ensures smooth data management and processing.

# Scalable Personalization Techniques

Personalization at scale requires scalable techniques to deliver tailored experiences to a large customer base. **Here are some scalable personalization techniques:**

Machine Learning and AI: Utilize machine learning algorithms and artificial intelligence (AI) to analyze large datasets and extract insights at scale. Machine learning models can identify patterns, predict customer behavior, and automate personalization efforts. Implement AI-driven recommendation systems to deliver personalized product suggestions and content.

Dynamic Content Generation: Use dynamic content generation techniques to create personalized content at scale. Leverage CRM data to dynamically generate email templates, landing pages, or product descriptions tailored to individual customer preferences. Dynamic content generation saves time and effort while delivering personalized experiences.

Automated Campaign Personalization: Leverage automation tools to personalize campaigns at scale. Implement dynamic campaign templates that automatically populate with customer-specific content, such as names, product recommendations, or purchase history. Automate campaign execution and personalization based on customer segments or triggers.

Self-Service Personalization: Empower customers to personalize their experiences through self-service options. Provide customers with preference centers or user profiles where they can customize their communication preferences, interests, or content recommendations. Self-service personalization offloads some personalization tasks from your team while giving customers control over their experiences.

# Balancing Automation and Human Touch

While automation plays a vital role in personalization at scale, it's essential to balance it with a human touch to maintain authentic and meaningful customer interactions. **Here's how to strike the right balance:**

Personalized Customer Support: Provide personalized customer support through various channels, including live chat, email, or phone. Train your support team to understand customer preferences and previous interactions, enabling them to provide personalized assistance. Combining automation with human support ensures a personalized and empathetic customer experience.

Personalized Outreach: Balance automated communication with personalized outreach efforts. Use automation for transactional or repetitive communications, such as order confirmations or shipping notifications. For more significant customer interactions, such as loyalty program milestones or personalized offers, consider personal outreach through phone calls, handwritten notes, or video messages.

Feedback and Relationship Building: Actively seek customer feedback and leverage it to build stronger relationships. Use automation to gather feedback through surveys or feedback forms, but also ensure personal follow-ups to address concerns or gather more insights. Building personal relationships fosters trust and loyalty.

Continuous Evaluation and Optimization: Continuously evaluate and optimize your personalization efforts to strike the right balance between automation and the human touch. Monitor customer feedback, engagement metrics, and conversion rates to gauge the effectiveness of your personalized marketing strategies. Adjust and optimize your approach based on customer preferences and evolving needs.

### *Conclusion:*

Personalization at scale requires efficient management of large customer databases, scalable personalization techniques, and a balanced approach between automation and the human touch. By implementing strategies to manage data effectively, leveraging scalable personalization techniques, and maintaining authentic customer interactions, businesses can successfully deliver personalized experiences to a growing customer base. In the final chapter, we will summarize the key takeaways and

discuss the future of personalized marketing strategies with
CRM.

# Chapter Nine

# OVERCOMING CHALLENGES AND PITFALLS

## Data Privacy And Ethical Considerations

Personalized marketing strategies heavily rely on customer data, which raises important considerations regarding data privacy and ethics. **Here are some key challenges and strategies for overcoming them:**

Compliance with Data Protection Regulations: Stay informed and comply with data protection regulations, such as the General Data Protection Regulation (GDPR) or the California Consumer Privacy Act (CCPA). Ensure that your data collection, storage, and usage practices align with the requirements of these regulations to protect customer privacy.

Transparent Data Practices: Be transparent about your data practices by clearly communicating how customer data is collected, stored, and used. Obtain explicit consent from customers for data collection and provide them with options to manage their preferences. Transparency builds trust and confidence among customers.

Data Security Measures: Implement robust data security measures to safeguard customer data against unauthorized access or breaches. Use encryption, access controls, and regular security audits to protect customer information. Prioritize data security as a fundamental aspect of your personalized marketing strategy.

# Managing Customer Expectations

When implementing personalized marketing strategies, managing customer expectations is crucial to avoid potential dissatisfaction. **Here's how to effectively manage customer expectations:**

Clear Communication: Set clear expectations with customers about the extent of personalization they can expect. Communicate how their data will be used to enhance their experience and emphasize the value they will receive. Be transparent about the limitations of personalization to avoid overpromising and underdelivering.

Opt-In and Opt-Out Options: Provide customers with opt-in and opt-out options for personalized marketing communications. Respect their preferences and ensure that they have control over the type and frequency of personalized messages they receive. Giving customers the ability to customize their experiences enhances satisfaction and engagement.

Customization Versus Intrusion: Strike the right balance between customization and intrusion. Avoid being overly intrusive or intrusive. Respect customer boundaries and use personalization techniques that enhance their experience without making them feel uncomfortable or overwhelmed.

# Avoiding Personalization Mistakes

While personalized marketing can be powerful, it's important to avoid common mistakes that can undermine its effectiveness. **Here are some pitfalls to avoid:**

Overreliance on Automation: While automation is valuable, don't solely rely on automated processes. Incorporate human judgment and intervention when necessary to ensure that personalization efforts are accurate, relevant, and empathetic.

Lack of Testing and Optimization: Don't overlook the importance of testing and optimization. Continuously test different personalization strategies, messages, and content variations to identify what resonates best with your target audience. Use A/B testing, analyze results, and optimize your campaigns accordingly.

Neglecting the Customer Journey: Personalization should be applied throughout the entire customer journey, from initial awareness to post-purchase interactions. Avoid focusing solely on the pre-purchase phase and neglecting personalization efforts in subsequent stages. Continuously personalize the customer experience to foster long-term relationships.

*Conclusion:*

Implementing personalized marketing strategies comes with challenges and potential pitfalls. By addressing data privacy and ethical considerations, managing customer expectations, and avoiding common personalization mistakes, businesses can navigate these challenges and ensure successful personalized marketing campaigns. In the final chapter, we will recap the key learnings and discuss the future of personalized marketing strategies with CRM.

# Chapter Ten

# MEASURING SUCCESS AND OPTIMIZING STRATEGIES

## Key Performance Indicators (Kpis) For Personalization

Measuring the success of personalized marketing strategies is essential for evaluating their effectiveness and making data-driven decisions. **Here are key performance indicators (KPIs) to consider:**

Conversion Rate: Measure the percentage of customers who take a desired action, such as making a purchase, completing a form, or subscribing to a service. Analyze the conversion rate for personalized campaigns compared to non-personalized campaigns to assess the impact of personalization on driving conversions.

Customer Engagement: Track customer engagement metrics, such as click-through rates, time spent on site, or social media interactions. Evaluate how personalized campaigns improve customer engagement compared to generic campaigns. Higher engagement indicates that personalization resonates with customers.

Customer Lifetime Value (CLV): Assess the impact of personalization on customer lifetime value. Measure the CLV of customers who have experienced personalized campaigns versus those who have not. Higher CLV for personalized customers indicates the effectiveness of personalization in fostering long-term customer relationships.

Customer Satisfaction: Gather customer feedback to measure satisfaction levels. Use surveys, ratings, or reviews to assess how personalized experiences impact customer satisfaction. Higher satisfaction scores indicate that personalization efforts meet or exceed customer expectations.

# Testing and Iterating Personalized Campaigns

Continuous testing and iteration are vital for optimizing personalized campaigns and maximizing their effectiveness. **Here's how to approach testing and iteration:**

A/B Testing: Conduct A/B tests to compare different variations of personalized campaigns. Test different elements, such as subject lines, content, offers, or call-to-action buttons. Analyze the results to identify the most effective elements for driving customer engagement and conversions.

Segmentation Testing: Test different customer segments to identify which segments respond best to specific personalization strategies. Determine the most effective personalization tactics for each segment, tailoring campaigns accordingly. Segmentation testing allows for more targeted and impactful personalization efforts.

Feedback Analysis: Analyze customer feedback, comments, and reviews to gain insights into the effectiveness of personalized campaigns. Identify common themes, pain points, or areas of improvement. Use this feedback to refine and iterate your personalization strategies based on customer preferences and needs.

# Continuous Improvement of CRM Strategies

To stay ahead in the ever-evolving landscape of personalized marketing, continuous improvement of CRM strategies is essential. **Here are some strategies for continuous improvement:**

Data Analysis: Continuously analyze customer data to uncover patterns, trends, and insights. Identify new opportunities for personalization, refine segmentation strategies, and discover emerging customer preferences. Data analysis provides the foundation for informed decision-making and strategic improvements.

Technology Evaluation: Regularly evaluate your CRM system and other marketing technologies to ensure they align with your evolving needs. Stay updated on the latest advancements in CRM technology, automation tools, and analytics platforms. Consider investing in new solutions that can enhance your personalization efforts.

Collaboration and Knowledge Sharing: Foster collaboration within your marketing team and across departments. Encourage knowledge sharing and cross-functional discussions to leverage diverse perspectives and insights. Regularly review and share best practices to drive continuous improvement in personalized marketing strategies.

Industry Research and Trends: Stay informed about industry trends, customer behavior shifts, and emerging technologies related to personalized marketing. Engage in industry research, attend conferences, and participate in relevant communities to stay up-to-date. Use this knowledge to adapt and optimize your CRM strategies accordingly.

***Conclusion:***

Measuring success, testing, iterating, and continuously improving CRM strategies are crucial for successful personalized marketing campaigns. By tracking key performance indicators, conducting A/B testing, analyzing customer feedback, and staying informed about industry trends, businesses can optimize their personalization efforts and drive better results. In the final chapter, we will summarize the key learnings and discuss the future of personalized marketing strategies with CRM.

# Conclusion:

In this book, we have explored the power of leveraging Customer Relationship Management (CRM) for personalized marketing strategies. We began by understanding the evolution of marketing from mass marketing to personalization, recognizing the importance of adapting to customer expectations and preferences in a highly competitive landscape.

We then delved into the foundations of CRM, defining its components and highlighting the benefits it offers for personalized marketing. CRM provides businesses with a comprehensive framework to manage customer interactions, gather valuable data, and deliver tailored experiences that resonate with individual customers.

Implementing a CRM system requires careful consideration, and we discussed the process of selecting the right CRM solution, integrating it with existing systems, and ensuring robust data management and security. A well-implemented CRM system forms the backbone of personalized marketing efforts, enabling businesses to collect, store, and utilize customer data effectively.

Building customer profiles is a critical step in personalization, and we explored various strategies for gathering customer data, segmenting customers based on their attributes and behaviors, and creating comprehensive customer profiles. These profiles serve as a foundation for developing personalized marketing campaigns that address specific customer needs and preferences.

With a solid foundation in place, we dived into the practical aspects of leveraging CRM for personalization. We explored techniques for customizing product recommendations, tailoring marketing messages, and enhancing the overall customer experience. By leveraging CRM capabilities, businesses can deliver personalized content, offers, and interactions that foster deeper engagement and drive customer loyalty.

Harnessing data analytics is another key aspect of effective personalized marketing. We discussed the importance of analyzing customer behavior, employing predictive analytics to anticipate customer needs, and using CRM insights to make data-driven marketing decisions. By leveraging data analytics, businesses can gain valuable insights into customer preferences and behavior, allowing for more targeted and effective personalization strategies.

Automation and workflow optimization play a crucial role in scaling personalized marketing efforts. We examined the importance of streamlining marketing processes, automating campaign management, and optimizing workflows to maximize efficiency and productivity. Automation enables businesses to deliver personalized experiences at scale, saving time and resources while maintaining consistency and relevance.

The power of omnichannel marketing was also explored, emphasizing the integration of multiple channels, creating consistent customer experiences across touchpoints, and orchestrating personalized campaigns that seamlessly span different platforms. By leveraging an omnichannel approach, businesses can provide customers with a cohesive and personalized journey, increasing engagement and driving conversions.

Personalization at scale presents its own set of challenges, and we discussed strategies for managing large customer databases, employing scalable personalization techniques, and striking the right balance between automation and the human touch. By effectively managing data, implementing scalable personalization techniques, and maintaining authentic customer interactions, businesses can successfully deliver personalized experiences to a growing customer base.

We also addressed the challenges and pitfalls associated with personalized marketing. We highlighted the importance of data privacy and ethical considerations, managing customer expectations, and avoiding common personalization mistakes. By proactively addressing these challenges, businesses can build trust, maintain customer satisfaction, and ensure the ethical use of customer data.

Measuring the success of personalized marketing strategies is crucial for optimization and decision-making. We discussed key performance indicators (KPIs) for personalization, testing and iterating personalized campaigns, and continuously improving CRM strategies. By tracking relevant metrics, analyzing customer feedback, and staying abreast of industry trends, businesses can refine their personalized marketing efforts and drive better results.

As we conclude this book, it is evident that CRM is a powerful tool for personalized marketing strategies. It empowers businesses to understand and connect with customers on a deeper level, delivering tailored experiences that resonate and drive meaningful engagement. However, personalization is an ongoing journey, and the future holds exciting opportunities for further innovation and advancement in CRM strategies.

By staying agile, embracing emerging technologies, and prioritizing customer-centricity, businesses can unlock the full potential of CRM for personalized marketing. The key lies in striking the right balance between automation and the human touch, leveraging data-driven insights, and continuously optimizing strategies based on customer needs and preferences.

With a strong foundation in CRM and personalized marketing, businesses can differentiate themselves in the competitive landscape, foster lasting customer relationships, and achieve sustainable growth. The power of CRM lies in its ability to transform customer interactions into meaningful experiences, and by harnessing this power, businesses can embark on a journey of personalized marketing success.

As technology evolves and customer expectations continue to shift, the principles and strategies discussed in this book will serve as a solid framework for businesses to navigate the ever-changing landscape of personalized marketing. With the right CRM system, data-driven insights, and a customer-centric approach, businesses can create personalized experiences that captivate customers, drive conversions, and build long-term loyalty.

The possibilities are limitless when it comes to leveraging CRM for personalized marketing. It is up to businesses to embrace this potential, adapt to the evolving needs of their customers, and make personalized experiences an integral part of their marketing strategies. The journey towards personalized marketing starts here, and the future is bright for those who dare to explore its boundless opportunities.

# The End